High Dive
and other Poems

By the same author :
POLE STAR AND OTHER POEMS

High Dive

AND OTHER POEMS BY

Margaret Rhodes

ARUNDEL: LINDEN PRESS 1968

FOR M.M.P. AND E.S.R.

900000 05 8

First published 1968 *by the Linden Press, Fontwell, Arundel, Sussex. Printed in Great Britain.*

CONTENTS

The author's thanks for permission to reprint
certain of the poems included in this collection
are due to the Editors of Punch, the Cornhill
Magazine, Outposts, English, Homes and
Gardens, Good Housekeeping, The Lady,
Country Life, and the Countryman

Palms

Across the road two palm trees stand,
Not like the furred giants of Bordighera—with crests among
    the stars
Or in sunlight unfurling umbrellas of shade over a molten
    land—
But tatterdemalion, poor relation palms
Tossed by our northern gales, lopped by last winter's frost
Piecemeal, past hope, failure's familiars.
Yet on a windy night
When the moon rocks with the old moon in her arms
Down the road rustles the rattle of leaves
Light as shells stirred upon shingle by the tide
Or wainscot-scuttering of starlings in the eaves . . .
And I, O I am lost
Far beyond living landmarks of time and space.

This wind roisters across Cadiz; some other I
Knew once deep in the bone and so for ever
That sea-borne city's darkness, nightlong knew
The palm-fronds' grasshopper frenzy of castanets
Under a starless sky.
There was a sound too of distant drums
And suddenly altar-shining in the light
Of myriad candles—see, see where comes
The paso, step by muffled step, swaying above floating
    faces
And nightmare hoods of penitents, torch in hand;
Where Roman soldiers ride
Behind the Calvary, and the sacta arrow of song wings
    down
Wringing, rinsing the heart, plumbing all grief.

7

There are places
Mirage-fading, known in a dream and forgotten on waking,
And others whose bland
And shuttered countenance like the face of a lover
Turns with a Mona Lisa smile, seeking
A sign, promising passion and peace and belief.
Almost one forgets
Until a wind clatters two workaday palms
In bird-brittle morse-message on a moon's night
And clear as the scenes of childhood to a crone's view
Are the sea and the sky cradling Cadiz in their arms.

Mistral

POLTERGEIST wind that from a cloudless sky
Rides Provence like a Fury—
Have you come from the grey reaches of the Rhône
Or pinnacles of Ventoux, from the eagle's eyrie?
You that with hooligan buffoonery
Pluck air bare as a bone,

Leprechaun-light, vaulting, vaunting your power
In gusts of wild mockery;
Flay cypresses that shield the countryside
And stalwart still against wind's trickery
Guard almond and vine and olive, for the hour
Of summer's apex, harvest-tide.

Tease, freakish wind, that when at last all's spent—
Puck's humour and behaviour—
Old men under the plane trees in the square
May once again play boule when day is over,
And by the fountain sit, warm with content
In green twilight there.

9

Shoppers

LIKE gulls on the wind the women came flying,
Their skirts billowing, winged willy-nilly, each passer-by
Leaning on the storm and crying
With a bird's cry.

Wheeling in from the harbour came the clouds of birds
Spindrift in their eyes, spreadeagled breasting the crest of
   the hill :
Only the anchoring baskets, above the wind's words,
Proclaimed them earthbound still.

Mont Hérault: An elegy

PAUSE for a moment here;
Here where the cliff falls away in a tawny landslip
Tangle of gorse and bracken broken sheer,
Reeling with gulls' cries;
No foothold, only precarious eternity
Between cliff edge and kingfisher-feathered sea.
Pause for a little space,
Dwell on each feature, fasten to memory
Colour and contour, this the last of earth's scenes
To be mirrored in her eyes.

The merciful tide has flowed where she was lying;
Warm with the texture of sunlight the coast leans
Halfway to heaven, but never again the same:
Whisper of terror troubles still a place
No longer anonymous, but echoing the sound of her name;
No more serene, but piteous with her dying.

The Alhambra, Granada

Cool as anemones in the sea's twilight glade
Lie courts delicately pillared, whorled like shells
Echoing in an underwater shade
The alien sound of bells;

And the air scalloped with falling fountains, fluted
With the arpeggio notes of waterfalls
Challenges noonday's sun; here all is muted
Within these empty halls.

Below this bubble, this amber bauble of Time
That Time has left untouched upon its hill,
The stalwart, coralline walls and towers climb—
A Moorish legend still—

Patined like an apricot ripening in the sun
Of a long summer, its kernel topaz-bright
With ancient splendour, fragile as cobweb spun
In arabesques of light.

Imagination flowers in stone, filigree
And stalactite most meticulously wrought,
Arched with those clustering honey-cells the bee
With waxen combs once taught.

Is all a fable? and do the myrtles lean
Above the pool in dreams? A mirador
Is pinnacled above the Albaicín :
And as from a far shore

Sounds beat upon the ear, borne from the throng
That peoples a strange city, a hive's hum
Belying fantasy : at a snatch of song
The centuries are dumb.

12

Perspective

SUDDENLY I remembered how the mountains of home
Would lie under the hunter's or harvest moon
Shellpale and passionless, shadowed like shifting dune
Or desert veined and ribbed by the wind's tide
And plucked into peak and crater at a whim.
I see them still
Shawled in a mist of moonlight; the dark Cwm
Splaying the mountainside,
Climbing from fields to the Druids' coven of stones;
Curve and contour of each fold and hill,
Trees storm-sculptured into a frieze of flight,
Valleys a waterfall of shadow.
                              Remembered, remote
Are the dove-breasted hills that ever brood over night,
Becalmed in time, soundless and mindless and mute,
Their beauty piercing the heart, because life's span
But pricks eternity, so frail is man.

Truant

THE little clouds in fair flocks went
Across the dappled firmament;
As swift, as silent as a sigh
They scaled the pathways of the sky
And mounted, cool and cobweb-light,
The far, unfathomable height.

And I, the pattern of whose days
Has followed no uncharted ways,
Who dust and polish while birds sing
And turn out cupboards in the Spring—
I stood bereft of sense or words
To see bird-clouds and white cloud-birds.

And so my caged and cumbered mind
Ran with the clouds before the wind
The whole day long . . . then pitched its tent
High in the star-strown firmament.
And there its sits and laughs aloud
Upon the battlements of cloud.

Ebb-Tide

THE grass-green water gleams like glass
And curls across the winter sand;
Feather-to-foam the white gulls pass
Tide-tossed towards the leafless land.

Here the bright children run and leap
Lighter than larks, and sing for joy;
The seaweed harvest theirs to reap,
Each carved and whorléd shell their toy.

Enchanted by the fitful sun
And heaven-high pinnacles of cloud,
On feet as free as air they run
Before the wind, and laugh aloud.

They have flung off all yesterdays;
Time is stood still for them; they hold
It captive in their candid gaze :
And as a new tale to be told

They look wide-eyed upon to-morrow.
These are our high hope to the last—
The fair future, for which we borrow
A little faith to keep steadfast.

The grass-green water frets the shore
And ripples run across the sand :
The children with their flotsam store
Run laughing to the waiting land.

15

Reservoir

Here was a green valley
Where cows stood fetlock-deep in quiet meadows,
And lichened oaks even on a midsummer noon
Stippled the lanes with sunlight and leaf-shadows.

Here in the cool morning
Birds sang, the air dissolved and muted
Into those liquid notes spilled from the trees . . .
All the birds of summer whistled and piped and luted.

The farms of hewn granite
With orchard and cider-press, by storm and centuries
                                                    weathered,
Stood serene in their fields; and over the long years
Passed from old men to stalwart sons they fathered.

All now is drowned for ever :
The lost lane leads to the water, and none follows;
No ripple marks its path.   On the far shore
Old bridle-paths emerge like ghosts from the shallows.

And where there were flowers—
Bugle and meadowsweet, honeysuckle hedges
And sweetbriar filling the warm, evening air—
Are only floating lilies beyond the sedges.

Now, from among the rushes
Watching the fish rise, and sea-gulls' shadows winging
Mirrored with clouds; soft as a sigh I hear
From branches beneath the water, the birds still singing.

Afternoon

I FOUND my love asleep
Where sun and shade lay deep
Under a leafy bough,
So that from throat to brow
Familiar features wore
A guise not known before,
And fathom-drowned in rest
Breath stirred not the warm breast.

Then terror like an arrow
Sped straightway through my marrow,
Too mortal woe for weeping . . .
Yet was my love but sleeping :
And like a tired child
Turned to me then, and smiled.

Shield

Under the fragile, tender curve of sky
Wind-lulled they walk, companioned by content,
And all the sweet delights of summer lie
Still warm upon them, now that summer's spent.

The children wander in a world of dreams
In squirrels' byways; they are for ever a part
Of secret spinneys and little singing streams . . .
For ever their clear voices pluck the heart.

Theirs is a world complete, robust, unscarred,
Springing with fountains of song and meadow flowers,
With swift enchantment strown; a world not marred
By any shadow on the sunlit hours.

We see them step bird-light beneath the trees
And, pierced by love, perceive that ever after
We, who would lap and fold them round with peace,
Can give alone courage, and faith, and laughter.

Under a Roof of Stars

I led my youngest child last night
Beneath the silver-swarming sky,
Through pools of shadow on the lawn,
To see the woolly clouds run by

And learn the lovely names of stars
That light a candle in the mind—
Orion, Sirius, Gemini—
Bright in their universe of wind.

I showed where branches fret the sky
And where night blooms with secret flowers,
And fruits of the Hesperides
Shine in the dark like boggart fires.

It was another earth last night.
The child looked up and laughed aloud
To see the world so strange and new
Under a roof of stars and cloud.

———

I dare not walk the unlighted lane
Or wander in the lonely wood,
And when night presses round the house
I am afraid of solitude.

While she, whose face is innocence,
Has never learnt the name of fear;
She counts the stars among her friends,
The darkness is a cloak to wear;

She sees no ambush in the trees
That shadow field and byre and farm . . .
And O, when childhood's past, may she
Walk in a world that's safe from harm.

19

Elixir

He who has known love
Has a fire to warm him;
World's inconstancy
Can no more harm him
Who has been one with stars,
Walked on the wind,
And scanned the far ranges
Of mortal mind.

His are the lost ways
Where none comes after,
Grasshopper-light he goes:
His speech is laughter.
And there pirouetting
Is the shadow of splendour,
While the earth about him
Grows green and tender.

Sea-Spell

I have lived always hearing the sound of the sea,
Pondering the wonder of its ways, matching its mood
Of sombre splendour and cloud-light revelry,
And known its wild, gull-haunted solitude.

Now I am one with the sea; no matter where
Inland I wander I hear its surge and swell,
Like distant breakers ravishing still the ear—
Spun from a whorled and water-whispering shell.

21

Wayfarer

Child, with the candid eyes
And kitten-curling hair,
That in the long grass lies
Sublimely unaware

That life can offer more
Than meadow starred with flowers,
Than ripple-rounded shore
Or dandelion-blown hours;

Child, with the tender ways,
What journey do you make
In sleep's most tortuous maze :
And with tears awake?

Elegy in Spring

What knife-edge of agony must mind have known,
What heart's abyss opening, that none could share
The torment of terror stretched too taut to bear
In a world quenched and like a dark wood grown
Peopled by shapes and shadows, where alone
She plumbed the awful ultimate of despair.
How could the mild and milky morning wear
Such a cheat's mien of grace, when hope had flown?

The eyes are windows for the self within;
There nightmare sits and pale illusions brood,
And yet none saw the face and form of dread
Moving behind the shutters . . . saw begin
Fear's avalanche, when she in solitude
Stretched out her hand and snapped life's tender thread.

23

Night Life

When the moth dusk draws down
To the candle flame
Of London Town
And the myriad tapers of light
Shine like a Milky Way;
Then, in the lingering, coralline flush of day
A city's starlings come
With a hubbub of wings, and the air dark with their flight.
Home in the bat-light, home
To Trafalgar Square, to column and arch and ledge
With voices heard above the roar of the Strand
In that cold no-man's-land
Of cornice and pilaster, crowded razor-edge,
Perch most precarious above the passers-by.
Vociferous, ruffled and round
Familiar feathery shapes that cluster high
Etched on the tapestry of night—
O starlings homeward bound
For Piccadilly's bright cloud-cuckoo-land :
Yours is the sound
Of London's voices filling all the sky.

On Winter Evenings

On winter evenings when I sit alone
While the house sleeps
Cradled and lulled and stilled, day's discord done,
Then mouse-soft silence creeps
On furred and timid feet beside my chair
And crouches suppliant there.

Children asleep now without stir or sigh
No echo send
Of high bird-voices; solitude and I
Share the bleak watch and commune friend to friend.
Turn softly, see, the future's mirrored here
And age is cameo-clear.

Moors in Spain

The Moors loved water, hearing in their dreams
Its speech, impersonal, remote, and cool :
Fountains' plainsong, the jocular sound of streams,
Sibilance of ripples fanned across a pool;
And waking to the chaffinch notes of rills
Tumbling incessantly from stair to stair.
They plumbed earth's deepest springs, whose water spills
Cool as sierra's snow on burning air;
An eastern fable flowered at their hand
In pillared courts and groves of cypress trees,
A little world of singing birds, a land
Within a land, of liquid harmonies.
Those fountains still, while centuries flow by,
Echo for ever Boabdil's last sigh.

Summer Evening

A woman in mauve sits at an open window
Above the shuttered shops and slattern street
Where lovers lean to each other under the archway
Oblivious in a kiss to sauntering feet
And drifts of orange peel and tattered paper . . .
She sits above, withdrawn in the shadowed room,
A moonpale face wavering between curtains
Watching the warm dusk bloom.

Now, by a trick of light or a quirk of fancy,
For a moment she glows—dark eyes and apricot skin—
Passionately transformed, leaning through a noon of flowers
To open the lattice and let evening in.
Fold close this hour, when the ebb-tide of summer
Shifting uncovers the bones of a drowned town
Where swirling canyons plunge between the houses
And a woman in mauve looks down.

Anniversary

You are that other I
Heart-harboured and long known
With passionate constancy,
Each into other grown
Each to other bound
In flesh and nerve and bone;
You are that other mind
I have put on,
Self within self,
Being's utmost horizon.
Fashioned whole from half,
Identity none
But what together we have
Being one :
I am that you, my love,
Chorus and antiphon.

Island at Evening

Sun falling behind the Martello tower
Holds rock and ripple folded in a calm,
The headland lightly limned in bat's colour
In dove or pigeon hues, engraved upon a sea
Of wrinkled silkskin puckered by a breath;
A sea the shade of its anemones,
Patterned with floating gulls dark on its petal-pallor :
For this is the gulls' hour.
Home at evening, threading the sun's path,
Sleek feathered boats their bodies cradled on the bay,
Swinging with the tide in the land's lee
Lulled home at evening; gulls, calling and keening
Where oars dip in darkling water, until gull and man
Are shadows, nothing more.
Now island swims in hyacinthine seas
As night moves over the beaches, outward from the shore,
And the moon draws itself from the water, leaning
On a cloud that mirrors the last light of day.
It is good the day should end as it began
And close so, on a psalm.

Jetsam

The cat came in at the door on a puff of wind,
Veiled the wildness of winter's stars that burned in its eyes,
Pausing, just over the threshold, to look behind
At clouds and broomsticks scudding across the skies.

Then, stepping delicately into a pool of light
Deceitfully domestic, enigma clothed in fur
It rubbed against a chair; remote, polite,
Stroking the air with a warm and feathery purr.

"It's company", she said, "not to be alone any more
In the empty house; it stands between me and the desert
                                                    places
Where solitude snuffles in darkness outside the door,
And pressing against the window are dead faces.

"It's company", she said; and the little cat lay curled
Artless as a baby, the pink pads of its paws
Stretched to the fire; alone in all the world
Between her and the abyss, her and those waiting jaws.

The Candle

Christmas is a golden candle
Set solitary in the heart
As on a dark window-sill some winter's night
Lonely with stars and frost.
It is a sign to all who are lost:
To lovers who have been long apart,
To the homeless and hopeless of all the earth,
To the old who hold out their arms to death.
It is a light for the bountiful and blest:
For the mother awaiting the hour of birth,
The father who would dandle
Love on his lap in the firelight;
And alike for saint and child
To whom every candle is a miracle.

In Praise of Daughters

Nothing can ever compare with daughters :
Spilling over with laughter, whispering on stairs,
Calling from room to room
With soaring choirboy voices; singing to-morrow's songs
And wearing popinjay top-of-the-morning colours
So that the house seems to bloom.
Theirs is the confident face the future wears
Only for the young; only to them belongs
Cockcrow and mayday, the rosy meadows of dawn;
They walk in the very climate of content.
About them is a casual holiday air,
And where they have been
Nothing is the same, even silence is aware :
Their warmth remains, and an echo of merriment.

Growing Pains

This little thistledown cat, frolicking
At follow-my-leader with its playfellow tail
Hugs to itself the sunlight, rollicking
In quicksilver capers; it is a tumble of fur
Light as a feather on the wind; as soft, as frail.

How can it learn in sleekly feline fashion
The panther's secret mien, and the queenly caveat—
This scuffle of flailing paws in infant passion,
This scrap of a kitten, all innocence and purr,
This little thistledown cat?

Harvest Home

The winging spire is a landmark; the bell calls
Across fields placid with cows; it swings and swells
To the land's rim, cliff crumbling to sea
And the mocking gulls.
It is an austere church, and gives no sign
Of the abundance, the glory of plenty within.
The pulpit sails upon a wave of flowers
And the deep window-sills
Cradle the fullness of harvest and husbandry :
Apples, smooth-cheeked and buffed to glowing rose,
Grapes with the moth's bloom warm upon them yet,
Mushrooms, cool and pale as milk,
Gathered from shadowy fields in the hour before dawn;
And in pride of place
A clutch of brown flecked eggs, homely in straw
Edged with a frill of parsley's frothy lace.
Here is the harvest bread, plaited in ears of corn,
And bursting figs, nectarines sleek as silk;
An autumn-coloured store
Fondly set out : love's true, traditional debt.
It is an austere church, the holy house
Of country people, stolid in their ways,
Considered in their giving, slow to rouse . . .
And poets in their praise.

Points of View

We saw tawny palaces, towers and campaniles
And spires soaring to heaven at a bound :
The child saw only a lizard as still as a stone
Sunning itself on the ground.

We saw white houses with filigree balconies
Spilling a summer of flowers in the sleeping heat :
The child saw a tousled song-bird in a cage
Above the narrow street.

We saw groves of olives and the gnarled fingers of vines
And noonday shimmering like water on the road :
The child saw only a donkey's plodding hooves
Beneath its panniered load.

We came reluctant home, to wrest weeds from the garden,
To open the windows and chivvy cobwebs from the house :
But the child came singing, wild with anticipation,
Back to a tame white mouse.

Remembering my Father

I think of you always at Aber;
And remembering Aber, I number
The long years of childhood, the years
That stretched once, an interminable span
Orderly, colourless, confined;
Years of walks on Sundays and wool next the skin,
The cumbersome, smothering trappings, the trouble and
                                                        clobber
Of growing up.
                    But you above all, you I remember
Lying with hands under your head, loving the sun,
Following the fronded path where hart's-tongues grew,
Aware of clouds and streams and trees and wings
And the pavane of the appointed spheres.
You taught a child to drink at secret springs;
Now, from a cairn of years
I remember you and the child : myself and you :
And the delicate bridge that linked me to your mind.

For my Father

I have been back at last: and you not there.
It was a spun-silk day of green and blue,
The landscape spread like a quilt
Patterned with hills and fields and trees and sheep
As I have seen it, waking and asleep,
Inseparable from every thought of you.

The years of childhood like a cloud of birds
About me troubled the air;
I came unwilling, not so much to seek
For you in memories prodigally spilt
As to confirm your going, accept my need.
Your books were there, a letter in the place
Where Death had tapped you on the shoulder;
And, underlined in pencil, the last words
Your mind had marked, so that to read
Was to hear you speak:
But of you no lightest touch, no echo, no trace.

Yet always when I look in a mirror I see
Now, growing older,
Your eyes in my own face look back at me.

Jamaican with an Umbrella

Crossing the street beneath a black umbrella,
His sober coat bespattered with Brixton rain,
He walks with the stride of a giant, eyes unseeing,
Past pram and poodle, kiosk and paperseller,
Grocer and butcher and cobbler and tombstone-maker,
Lost in a dream of sun : for never again
Will the sun itself take root in the core of his being.
Yet even in passing by
He scatters a sort of brightness over the day,
A sunburst of poster colours, a kingfisher sky;
And fronded palms fringe the shores of far Jamaica
As under a black umbrella he goes his way.

Harbour in Winter

A harbour should be seen on a winter's morning,
The tide low, and leggy shadows leaning
Across the wrinkled sands where seablown birds
Stilt-walk along the water's fringe of wrack and weed,
And wind scrambles their cries with bells, waves, words.
Beyond storm's claws boats tilt on the dry sea-bed
And natty sandpipers dance to their own keening.

Not in the summer, plump and sleek with dreaming,
Not in the hum of summer, the sunlight teeming
With patchwork of sails and boats in holiday mood,
A jostle of yachts and dinghies and lubber laughter . . .
A harbour needs winter and winter's solitude,
And a shoal offshore, with gulls dive-bombing after
As back they wheel on the wind, to the harbour homing.

Harbour in Summer

A gaggle of yachts fan out, wings spread to the wind;
And gosling dinghies fuss and scurry about
On the motor launches' swell,
Ferrying families spruce in poster-colours,
In sailcloth of scarlet and royal and cinnamon yellow.
The sky of birds'-egg blue is an echoing shell,
The sun is a shout.

Folk fish; their shadows like sundials move
As the eyes of the floats below wink red and green.
They sit on the breakwater, silent, remote, serene
In a void of time, between before and after,
Held in the bubble of summer.
Waves chuckle, slapping and tickling each other,
Deceptive as lion cubs or a hurricane's eye;
Gulls stand on swaying masts to survey the scene—
And skim out to sea again with a screech of laughter.

First Swallow

First swallow of summer whose geometry of flight
Shears into shimmering particles the air,
In your invisible hieroglyphics write
News of the swarthy sunburned south : prepare
Our northern eyes for light.

We plot the pattern of your journeyings
And watch—awake to wonder like a child—
The skill of those precise and punctual wings
Nurtured on sunlight, on winters green and mild
And swift bright-bannered springs.

In every heart these keep a constant place :
Bells on a frosty night; the newborn cry;
Clouds; candles; spires; waves breaking; a loved face;
And the first swallow of summer in a clear sky
Bringing the sun's grace.

Child Fishing

Becalmed in the bay boats swing to the evening tide,
The sun plummets, trailing a scarf of mist,
And feathered as tender a pink as flamingoes, ripples fan
                                                        wide;
A sail is a silhouette, shadows are amethyst.

The child sits on a rock, remote, absorbed, intent,
Angling for crabs wily in the weeds of a pool,
Manoeuvring a limpet on a line, lost in entire content.
The moment is all; home does not exist, nor school.

Step softly over the ribs of sand as the sun goes down
In a fiery fleece, and seagulls stroll on the shore;
For to-night will be part of a life for ever: deep in the
                                                        bone
A strength and a succour when the child is a child no
                                                        more.

Old Tom

Nothing is jollier than a rollicking tom cat
When the sun tickles him—
Prancing stiff-legged round his own shadow,
Sillier than a springtime lamb in a meadow;
Scurrying up trees and teasing the leaves on the branches,
Following funny feline hunches,
Whirling like a dervish at a whim—
Zany old tom.

But look at him now, spreadeagled in dreamless sleep,
Paws furled, underbelly soft as a moth,
Curled in the very cipher of sloth;
Not for him the sprawling furry heap
Even in oblivion,
But the grace of a prima ballerina turned swan :
Until the sunlight suddenly tickles him—
Zany old tom.

High Dive

Intent, withdrawn, the child-face now severe,
Mind mastering each muscle, first she stands
Upon a pinnacle of loneliness; mustering strength,
Crystallizing purpose, solitary against summer's sky.
For a moment waits there while the voice of fear
Loosens her limbs, cajoling in her ear;
Then, resolute at length,
Taut, tense, with arrowing hands
Curves in a hawk-plunge, sun-doomed-Icarus hurled;
The blade that is her body slicing sheer
The water's haven, secret, sheltering.
And now the crowd applauds her with a sigh—
Rapt, without word
For flight without the succour of a wing.

To-day she has known the heart-beat of a bird
And learnt, today, the rhythm of a world.

Spring-Burst

Suddenly this morning Spring uncurled its fist
Spilling primroses on the still wintry earth;
Now, listen, listen to the small birds' mirth
Who have known only mocking flowers of frost
This long time past.
Hear now the hive of voices from the wood :
Rustle and stir, whisper of feather, coo, chirp, whistle,
Crackle of twig, the sounds of haste and hustle
Where winterlong all seemed a solitude;
And suddenly in flood
The thawed streams chuckle and crow,
Their banks soft-furred with moss instead of snow.

Boy and Kite

One with the wind he runs
And tugs a cloud upon a string;
His are the wheeling suns
In unseen galaxy,
The blue unfathomable sky,
His the eagle's wing.

Wind-light on upland grass
He scampers, whistles, laughs aloud
Heedless that time must pass,
That in his mind for ever
A boy will run through the clover
Tugging a captive cloud.

Between Seville and Jerez

Between Seville and Jerez moonlight was a lake
Lapping the empty road;
Each olive grew from the silver water
Like an old man paddling;
Each was a tree of seaweed or bone-white coral
With wavering underwater boughs.
It was the moon's night
Warm and windless, and silent as the Sargasso sea.
Once an owl swam through the air
His wings wimpling the mere of the sky,
And afterwards the cicadas woke
With their staccato grasshopper voices,
Querulous chimney-corner voices
Scraping across the night.
Then no mirage, but a moon's miracle!
A whitewashed cottage at the roadside
And two girls dancing, two spinning shadows
Arms raised, castanets snapping like the cicadas
With the rhythm of Spain; two girls dancing
Disciplined as ballerinas
With snakes' bodies and snapping fingers
Dancing on the shore of the lake of moonlight
On the road from Seville to Jerez, one night in Spring.

Hostages

The time comes when you can do no more.
Bid them set sail now,
Help them to push their boat out from the shore,
And stand in the shallows on the fretted sand
And wave your hand.

They have grown for this, waited many years;
They will not fail now.
On the horizon a sturdy sail appears;
Wave, wave and turn back to the shore,
You can do no more.

Spanish Donkey

I hope there is a heaven for Spanish donkeys
Plodding under the whiplash of the sun,
Their panniers bulging with humdrum workaday

                                            burdens—
Poor patient lackeys, poor disregarded flunkeys
Whose tasks are never done.

I hope there will come to each of them, some day,
Somewhere along that infinite chafing road
The sound of a stream, and a special angel to lead him
Into a meadow, and there on the new-mown hay
Let fall, at last, his load.

To a Cactus

Portly green pincushion that on my window-sill
Squats like a fat inflated frog; weird bulbous growth
Protuberant of paunch, suck up your fill
Of sunlight, you, epitome of sloth,

Devour the sunlight with a southern passion,
My vegetable hedgehog, against the hour
Of sudden beauty : when overnight you fashion
The triumph of your solitary flower.

Inheritance

Look first by moonlight; the pale façade
Seen through beechboughs, the watching windows
Unlidded, no lamp alight within
Nor fireflame pirouetting in the rooms:
Stand, here in the familiar garden shadows
Beyond the stippled lawn
And see how in moonlight the old house blooms.

There is nothing to add or to discard,
It is entirely right.
If there are ghosts here, it has taken them in,
Cradling them in its arms
With the quiet dead, and the living and the yet
unborn . . .
Look first at the house through beechboughs, some moon's
night.

51

Esther

Remember Esther, six swift years a wife,
Dying rebellious in the upstairs room
To bring twin boys to birth;
Seeing for the last time
The sky scored with branches, every star
Caught in a net of leaves,
Her world shrunk to a window;
For the last time
Hearing the small birds chatter in the eaves,
The distant bell, the last cockcrow;
Listening, stricken, to the newborn cry.
She, who so clung to life
That after death her spirit used to come
Again about her home,
Was suddenly no more than a shadow
Standing at the turn of the stair.
She had become a step at the nursery door—
Which opened to discover no one there—
A breath in the garden at evening, the gate ajar;
Or in winter, a sigh in the silence beside the hearth;
Poor Esther: nothing more.
Remember her, who knew this house as home
Two hundred years ago,
And was too young to die.

Need

I want to walk in the white moonlight on a thin rind of
beach
With dry crabs rustling in the pods and streamers of weed,
And long shadows for company; to-night I need
To hold out my arms to the just-out-of-reach.

I don't want to be a housewife any more—
Cleaning the silver, hanging out wind-crazy washing
On bleak and boisterous Mondays,
Going to the market, always cooking a roast on
Sundays . .
I want to walk like a moonghost on the shore.

Draw the curtains, close shutters fast against night,
Turn from the beckoning finger of pale light:
To-morrow will be safe, to-morrow will shelter and
enfold,
To-morrow I shall be old.

53

Punctuation

Poor, cold, inconsequential birds
Writing their hieroglyphic words
Across a wilderness of white!
I watch them in the bone-bleak light:
Dark pods on brittle stalks they go—
Full stops and commas in the snow.

A River

I wish I could live by the slow waters of the Dordogne
Under the picked bones of the Causses, tucked into a
                                  fold of hillside
In a house of the warm lion-coloured stone
Roofed with tiles like a drift of autumn leaves,
Crinkled and ribbed, burnished,
Tiles rubbed to a fine patina by wind and years;
A house that has grown into the countryside
With roots fast in the rich earth of Périgord.
There would be the shade of walnut and chestnut trees,
A small vineyard sloping to the sun,
Maize and tobacco drying under the eaves
And the neighbours' fields of sweet corn
Ripening in autumn.
The windows would open to the river:
I should hear water always, even in sleep,
And wake to birdsong, cockcrow, wheels creaking,
                                  buckets clanking,
All the proper morning noises;
And a man fishing below the window,
Casting easily towards the willows on the farther shore.
Beyond the shutters, my rickety balcony
Would be hung with scarlet creeper like a lei,
And there I would water my row of flower pots
Spilling over with geraniums and begonias and a pink
                                  oleander.
I could live out my years by the slow waters of the
                                  Dordogne.

Sandpipers

Natty city gentlemen wading in rocky pools,
Delicately picking their watery way
Over the sea's scum, the bladder-wrack and sea pods
The crab skeletons and cuttle shells,
All things brittle, sand-scored and scuttling, all
That the waves stir into being and let fall.
See them now, with a hint of furled umbrella
Pinstripes and briefcase, always hurrying
On their spindly stalks.
Why should they skim the beach with that running glide
Walking as one in a desperate hurry walks,
When their business is with the slow turn of the tide?
Beachcombing the pools and the wave's fringe
That sieves a treasure of shells.
Beachcombers dressed as natty gentlemen :
See them go, scurrying, chased by the wind—
Little and fussy, with needling beaks; and footfalls
That scribble a typical signature in the sand.
A flight of gulls screams in and they are flown
Flinging over their shoulders their farewells
In voices thin as underwater bells.

Experience

I have hung over the void
Turning this way and that in the wind
Gulls plucking at my eyes
The rock crumbling under my clutching fingers.
Far, far below the green and sluggish sea
Waited, spread out like a firemen's blanket
While the sun climbed the summer sky to noon;
Above, the cliff-top grasses stirred, so near
That when the wind for a moment lulled I'd hear
Them rustling there, yet worlds beyond my reach.
Far, far above the puffs of cloud sailed by;
Below, the placid and familiar beach
Lay empty as the mountains of the moon.
The sun made little suns behind my eyes,
The wind whittled me to a scarecrow,
My voice was drowned in the cauldron of gulls' cries.
Long, long I lay inhuman : how or where
At last you drew me from the greedy air
My love, I cannot guess;
How steadied the tilting horizon again for me
Snatched back from nothingness.

Encounter

This morning in sun I saw a cat walking,
A large ginger gentleman coming downhill
With stiff forelegs, very dignified.
Nothing of the dandy about him, nothing handsome
To take the eye on a fine-fettled morning,
Just a bit of old rug taking the air
On a hill in the steep part of the town.
Only the two of us there, one plodding upwards, one
                                            stalking
Down some stately invisible stair,
Scorning the human race and all its futile ways,
It would be impertinent to praise
An animal so cock-a-hoop with pride,
With not a purr to spare
For any poor two-legged nonentity;
But as we passed, this cat considered me,
Then glanced away : it was such a look as Samson
Must have turned upon his unseen enemies
Before he brought the pillars crashing down.

To an Absent Daughter, with Primroses

Dearest Child, I send you these primroses.
See, I have lined the box with moss from the Jaonnet
valley,
From the high bank studded with celandine
And flat green buttons of pennywort, butcher's broom
And ferns coiled like furred springs.
To-day, it seemed to be all primroses,
The fields were yellow with them, among the tree roots
They lay, translucent as shells;
The bone-bare branches wore a haze of green,
And across the valley birds called to each other,
And there was a sudden urgency of wings,
It was all there, your childhood; the country ways
That you remember, spring spilling over with flowers,
The long green days . . .
All this I send you, Child, with these primroses.
See, I have tucked in some wild violets,
And a few sticky buds to open in water:
A bunch of remembered days
Smelling of damp moss from the Jaonnet valley.

Martha

Forgive me, one of the Marthas of Your world
With a busy jack-in-the-box mind
Thinking of this and that,
Spilling over with bric-a-brac—schemes
And plans and rags and tatters of dreams.
One of the world's many Marthas
Needing three hands, eighty minutes in an hour,
Thirty hours in a day;
Always a little out of breath, running behind
The lolloping hours, trying to keep time at bay.
Never quite succeeding
In finding that stillness of the heart, in which Your voice
Is like falling water, or like the dawn wind.
Forgive me that I have not found time to be:
Curled round myself like a cat
Sunning itself on a wall: emptied: lying in wait
For a cloud, the shadow of a wing, or a flower.

Dear Lord, shake out the ragbag of my mind,
Let me pick it over in sunlight, and find
Scraps to fashion a patchwork like a stained-glass
                                                        window.
Forgive me and hear me;
It is one of the world's Marthas who is pleading.

Venice

All cities are a Saturnalia of sound:
Clip-clop of carozzas, bells swinging to the stars,
Cries of ubiquitous vendors of the lottery ticket,
A Sunday hurdy-gurdy churning round
To some time-worn refrain;
The endless cacophony of motor cars,
Police-whistle, train-clangour,
And tyres hissing on seal-sleek streets in rain . . .
The whole rip-roaring racket
Soars to a crescendo and bursts in the brain like anger.

Only Venice, matchless and doomed,
With its warm wild-honey-coloured palaces
Leaning narcissus-like upon waterways,
Is muted to a timeless mood
Chimeric, solemn.
At night, to one sitting in solitude
In the piazzetta, beneath the towered and rosy-domed
Fantasy of St. Mark's and the winged lion on its column,
The city's murmur is a madrigal.
There is the fretting and slapping of water in secret
                                        places,
A song from a gondola etched on darkness there;
And everywhere the moth-soft muffled
Sound of steps: swift stride, footfall,
Flurry and pad of footsteps to and fro
In slippered silence; and voices
Falling like pebbles in a pool, stifled
To a whisper in warm air.
The Bronze Moors strike the hour:
There is an echo of laughter, and suddenly violins play
From the piazza; and Venice unfolds like a flower.

61

Flight

How shall I lend my love to the luckless air,
Bid him godspeed in a strange element
Of wind's mockery, the feckless and debonair
Dolphins of cloud in heaven's continent?

How stem the storms that he will soon bestride
And lose him to the treacherous sky's alarms
Unless an angel eagles at his side
And underneath are everlasting arms.

Mirador

Here in Time's turret stand,
Watch how the sun strides, leaning to noon's meadow,
And cuts a swathe of shadow
Grape-black across the clamorous harsh land—
A benediction, a reprieve from light.
Beyond, Granada shimmers in the sun
Bleached of all colour, polished as a bone;
But here a frieze of fountains cools the sight
And cypresses create a midnight shade.
In poetry of stone
This filigree tower, this mirador was made
Once, as an eyrie for a Moorish queen.
Here cage-birds blithely whiled away the hours
Where women preened, and sang, and died for love,
And laughed, and were afraid
Among myrtles and secret waterfalls and flowers.

A Tree

When overnight the furled cherry buds break
Into a cloud of white butterflies against a blue sky,
And on a new-minted morning we wake
To the roocooing of pigeons;
Then always, then I remember my Father.

When I was young enough to hold his hand
He planted a flowering cherry at the gate.
Before, one Spring was like another:
Searching for the first violets in the lane,
Echoing the cuckoo, seeing the first swallow,
Making the first daisy chain,
Looking for lambs and birds' nests and pussy willow;
But now, each year, Spring was the cherry tree.
In the lull between breakfast and church at eleven
Every Sunday we went, my Father and I—
He whistling "Praise my soul the King of Heaven"—
And if Spring that year was late
We looked at the boughs of the cherry, and could not wait
To see them heavy with bloom like snow;
But the miracle always unfolded, for us to see.

I was too young, I did not understand
Half a lifetime ago
That having a child and planting a flowering tree
Is immortality.